PRODIGAL PARENT process WORKBOOK

Prodigal Parent Process
Copyright © 2021 by Douglas Weiss, Ph.D.

Requests for information:
Discovery Press
heart2heart@xc.org
719-278-3708

Interior and Cover designed by Janelle Evangelides

Printed in the United States of America
ISBN # 978-1-881292-45-6

No portion of this material may be reproduced in any form or by any means without written permission of the author.

Contents

Disc One:

SESSION ONE: INTRODUCTION (LENGTH: 2 MINUTES 39 SECONDS) — 6
SESSION TWO: THE FIRST PRODIGAL PARENT (LENGTH: 8 MINUTES 19 SECONDS) — 11
SESSION THREE: PRODIGAL AND GOD (LENGTH: 9 MINUTES 17 SECONDS) — 20
SESSION FOUR: PRODIGAL SON (LENGTH: 9 MINUTES 23 SECONDS) — 23
SESSION FIVE: PROBLEMS FOR THE PRODIGAL (LENGTH: 6 MINUTES 21 SECONDS) — 27
SESSION SIX: SECRET TRAUMA (LENGTH: 7 MINUTES 13 SECONDS) — 31
SESSION SEVEN: SEX (LENGTH: 5 MINUTES 46 SECONDS) — 33
SESSION EIGHT: PRODIGALS AND DISORDERS (LENGTH: 12 MINUTES 39 SECONDS) — 36
SESSION NINE: TRUST/MISTRUST (LENGTH: 11 MINUTES) — 39
SESSION TEN: THE WILL (LENGTH: 6 MINUTES 32 SECONDS) — 45
SESSION ELEVEN: OBJECT VS. RELATIONAL THINKING (LENGTH: 10 MINUTES 41 SECONDS) — 47

Disc Two:

SESSION ONE: STARTING YOUR PROCESS (LENGTH: 4 MINUTES 26 SECONDS) — 50
SESSION TWO: TRAUMA (LENGTH: 4 MINUTES 08 SECONDS) — 52
SESSION THREE: EVERYONE IS DIFFERENT (LENGTH: 7 MINUTES 24 SECONDS) — 55
SESSION FOUR: POST TRAUMATIC STRESS DISORDER (LENGTH: 11 MINUTES 42 SECONDS) — 59
SESSION FIVE: GRIEF (LENGTH: 20 MINUTES 05 SECONDS) — 63
SESSION SIX: ANGER (LENGTH: 9 MINUTES 37 SECONDS) — 70
SESSION SEVEN: FORGIVENESS (LENGTH: 8 MINUTES 34 SECONDS) — 73
SESSION EIGHT: CAUSE AND EFFECT (LENGTH: 5 MINUTES 14 SECONDS) — 75
SESSION NINE: POWERLESS (LENGTH: 5 MINUTES 53 SECONDS) — 78

Disc Three:

SESSION ONE: PROVERBS 22:6 (LENGTH: 8 MINUTES 14 SECONDS) — 80
SESSION TWO: ALMOST NEVER (LENGTH: 7 MINUTES 03 SECONDS) — 82
SESSION THREE: THE FATHER'S BEHAVIOR (LENGTH: 5 MINUTES 25 SECONDS) — 85
SESSION FOUR: BOUNDARIES (LENGTH: 8 MINUTES 26 SECONDS) — 89

SESION FIVE: THE SIBLINGS (LENGTH: 14 MINUTES 30 SECONDS	93
SESSION SIX: TAKING RESPONSIBILITY (LENGTH: 7 MINUTES 06 SECONDS)	97
SESSION SEVEN: FORGIVING US (LENGTH: 4 MINUTES 20 SECONDS)	102
SESSION EIGHT: BLAMING (LENGTH: 3 MINUTES 25 SECONDS)	104
SESSION NINE: THE MARRIAGE (LENGTH: 7 MINUTES 34 SECONDS)	107
SESSION TEN: MY HOPE (LENGTH: 6 MINUTES 27 SECONDS)	111

Introduction

As a Christian Psychologist, I've heard many parents of prodigals in my office share feelings of despair over the direction and path their prodigal has chosen to take.

All too often I hear these questions:

"How can I make my prodigal change?"
"What did I do to cause this?"
"How do I respond to my prodigal's behavior?"

My heart in creating this series is to therapeutically walk you through the answers to these common questions and so much more. By working through this workbook in conjunction with the DVD, you will be educated, prepared, and capable of working through this process as a parent of a prodigal.

Being a parent of a prodigal is not something you asked for. In fact, at this very moment, you may feel like you're going through an emotional roller coaster with your prodigal child. As I have worked with couples who are feeling grief, shame, depression, anxiety, and even PTSD symptoms because of their prodigal child's choices, I have come up with these therapeutic exercises and biblical teachings that can help you profoundly understand your prodigal's journey as well as your own.

I want to applaud you for walking through this journey with thousands of other prodigal parents who are in the process of awaiting their prodigal to come home.

Through this series, my goal is that you anchor yourself in the truth as it relates to your prodigal's free will and your healing process as a parent.

Douglas Weiss Ph.D.

Introduction

DISC ONE: SESSION ONE
LENGTH: 2 MINUTES 39 SECONDS

The story you are living is behind c_____ doors.

Prodigals can impact your:

    Your L_____

    Your M_____

    Your R_____

You are not a_____.

You can have f_____ for your prodigal to come back home.

This series will help you understand your g_____, your f_____, and help you walk through the parent prodigal process.

SESSION NOTES:

_____
_____
_____
_____
_____
_____
_____
_____
_____

Homework

As we discussed in this session, many parents of prodigals keep their prodigal story to themselves. It is important in your healing journey to share this story.

What are you hoping to gain from going through this series?

_____
_____
_____
_____

Write out your prodigal's story. (This is not your story but theirs.)

_____
_____
_____
_____
_____
_____
_____
_____
_____
_____
_____
_____
_____
_____
_____
_____

Write your story as a parent of a prodigal.

Read your story to your spouse. Have your spouse read their story to you (if applicable). What did you learn from hearing your spouse's story?

_____
_____
_____
_____
_____
_____
_____

If you are part of a Prodigal Parents Group, read each of your stories to the group. What did you gain by reading your story to your group and hearing other group member's stories?

_____
_____
_____
_____
_____
_____
_____
_____

At this point in your journey, who are the people that know about your prodigal outside of immediate family?

1._____   4._____

2._____   5._____

3._____   6._____

How often are you able to share your experiences and feelings about your prodigal with anyone outside of your immediate family?

_____

I want to encourage you as you go through the entire series. This series was created for you to experience understanding and healing along this Prodigal Parent Process. Each segment was created for a unique and therapeutic reason. As you work through the pages of this book, I pray that these Christian principles guide you as you navigate your marriage, family, and your relationship with your prodigal child.

The First Prodigal Parent

DISC ONE: SESSION TWO
LENGTH: 8 MINUTES 19 SECONDS

Have you ever considered that God is a prodigal parent? Not only is He a prodigal parent, but He was the first prodigal parent in existence! It's remarkable to have a perfect environment, perfect parent, and yet get a prodigal outcome. This could only happen with a variable of free will.

> *1* Now the serpent was more crafty than any of the wild animals the Lord God had made. He said to the woman, "Did God really say, 'You must not eat from any tree in the garden'?" *2* The woman said to the serpent, "We may eat fruit from the trees in the garden, *3* but God did say, 'You must not eat fruit from the tree that is in the middle of the garden, and you must not touch it, or you will die.'" *4* "You will not certainly die," the serpent said to the woman. *5* "For God knows that when you eat from it your eyes will be opened, and you will be like God, knowing good and evil." - Genesis 3:1-5 (NIV)

God gave Adam and Eve the p_____ environment in the garden.

The prodigal journey starts with d_____ God.

We live in a moral universe where choices have c_____.

You, like God, were a good parent and provided them a safe e_____.

The Father did not:

    T_____ R_____

    B_____ H_____

    Q_____ His P_____

B_____ the Holy Spirit

Make their sin H_____ Issue

According to Genesis 3, the prodigal's choice to disbelieve God and to disobey God is _____% the prodigal's and _____% the fault of the parent (God).

SESSION NOTES:
_____
_____
_____
_____
_____
_____
_____
_____
_____

Homework

As far as an environment, review how you went about creating an environment for your prodigal and other children.

Memories of creating a spiritual environment:
_____
_____
_____
_____
_____

Memories of creating a house/physical home:
_____
_____
_____
_____
_____
_____

Memories of creating fun:
_____
_____
_____
_____
_____
_____

Memories of giving them opportunities to grow:
_____
_____
_____
_____
_____
_____

Memories of giving physical things that were special to them:
_____
_____
_____
_____
_____
_____

Memories of being there for them emotionally during difficult times or times of celebration:

_____
_____
_____
_____
_____

Memories of supporting them with time - be it events or just quality time:

_____
_____
_____
_____
_____

The point in having you write out all of this is for you both to see that, as a parent, you did create an environment. Environment, even if it's the same for each child, sadly doesn't guarantee outcome.

What are some of the feelings and thoughts that come to mind when you think about the many years of planning, spending, serving, and pouring your heart and energy into your children?

_____
_____
_____
_____
_____
_____

The prodigal process usually starts with the prodigal doubting or disbelieving what God really said and questioning whether God is good. From your viewpoint, what was the beginning of the prodigal process like for your prodigal?

_____
_____
_____
_____
_____
_____
_____
_____

In Genesis 3:3, Eve quotes back exactly what God said, "But God did say 'you must not eat fruit from the tree that is in the middle of the garden and you must not touch it or you will die.'" Eve, and Adam for that matter, absolutely knew God's Word prior to choosing a prodigal process.

Give examples of you teaching God's Word to your prodigal:

_____
_____
_____
_____
_____
_____
_____

What are some truths or principles you intentionally taught your prodigal that really stick out to you?

1._____

2._____

3. _____
4. _____
5. _____

God (the first prodigal parent) responded with consequences to His children's behavior. What are your thoughts on this?

_____
_____
_____
_____
_____

Adam and Eve were escorted out of the garden as their consequence for disobeying God. Explain how this consequence was and is significant.

_____
_____
_____
_____

What are examples of boundaries and consequences you have set with your prodigal?

1. _____
2. _____
3. _____
4. _____
5. _____

In this session, when looking at the Father, I discussed what the Father did not do.

Write out your thoughts about each on of these ideas:

1. Take Responsibility:

___

2. Blame Himself:

___

3. Question His Parenting:

___

4. Blame the Holy Spirit:

___

5. Make their sin His issue:

___

Now I want you to evaluate and comment on each of these five points that the Father did not do in light of where you are currently on these ideas. Give yourself a grade A through F and comment on why you gave yourself that grade.

1. Did not take any responsibility for their choices: Grade:_____

_____
_____
_____
_____

2. Blame Himself: Grade:_____

_____
_____
_____
_____

3. Question His parenting: Grade:_____

_____
_____
_____
_____

4. Blaming others: Grade:_____

_____
_____
_____
_____

5. Make their sin His issue: Grade:_____

_____
_____
_____
_____

What are your thoughts about the fact that God didn't bail Adam and Eve out or rescue them from known consequences?

_____
_____
_____
_____
_____

What are some of your takeaways watching God as a prodigal parent?

1._____
2._____
3._____
4._____
5._____

Prodigal and God

DISC ONE: SESSION THREE
LENGTH: 9 MINUTES 17 SECONDS

If you understand the Prodigal Process it can help you:

1. D_____ the process

2. Know how to p_____

3. Not take f_____ responsibility

> Since what may be known about God is plain to them, because God has made it plain to them. - Romans 1:19 (NIV)

It's not that they don't know God, it's what they do with their k_____ of God.

> For although they knew God, they neither glorified him as God nor gave thanks to him, but their thinking became futile and their foolish hearts were darkened. - Romans 1:21 (NIV)

A prodigal is _____% about their personal relationship with God.

The Prodigal Process is not about r_____ you.

When a heart rejects God it becomes d_____.

The heart is where we b_____.

> ²² Although they claimed to be wise, they became fools ²³ and exchanged the glory of the immortal God for images made to look like a mortal human being and birds and animals and reptiles. - Romans 1:22-23 (NIV)

After a prodigal moves away from believing in God, the next step is to find s_____ else to believe in.

This process of not believing in God to believing in something else is r_____ of what kind of parent you are.

The Prodigal Process is an i_____ heart process not a f_____ process.

There is nowhere in scripture that blames the p_____ for the prodigal journey.

SESSION NOTES:

_____
_____
_____
_____
_____
_____
_____
_____

Homework

In Romans 1, Paul explains how God has made Himself known to all. So, it's clear that your prodigal knows God.

What are some examples of your son/daughter knowing God over the course of their life?

1. _____
2. _____
3. _____
4. _____
5. _____

What are the various ways you tried to instill a knowledge of God/Christ in your child's life.

1. _____
2. _____
3. _____
4. _____
5. _____

What examples do you have of your prodigal's "thinking becoming futile"?

1. _____
2. _____
3. _____
4. _____
5. _____

In this session, I discussed that your prodigal's process is not about rejecting you. How does this make you feel?

_____
_____
_____

What are some of the principles that you know your prodigal believes in?

1. _____
2. _____
3. _____
4. _____
5. _____

Prodigal Son

DISC ONE: SESSION FOUR
LENGTH: 9 MINUTES 23 SECONDS

In the story of the prodigal, there are several characters. This session focuses on the prodigal son.

> ¹¹ Jesus continued: "There was a man who had two sons. ¹² The younger one said to his father, 'Father, give me my share of the estate.' So, he divided his property between them. - Luke 15:11-12 (NIV)

Right away we are introduced to an e_____ young man.

The father was an o_____ not a soul for the prodigal to get what he wanted. Give examples of your feeling or actions being used by your prodigal.

The father allowed his son to use him and to use his free w_____.

> "Not long after that, the younger son got together all he had, set off for a distant country and there squandered his wealth in wild living." - Luke 15:13 (NIV)

When prodigals know they are going to do unacceptable, ungodly, or even wicked behavior they:

   1. Move away from anyone who is g_____.

   2. Move away from anyone with a_____ in their life.

   3. They shut f_____ members out.

The reason is that they have u_____ intentions in their heart.

The decision to be distant and act in ungodly ways are decisions of the h_____ that are carried out in behavior.

> ¹⁴ "After he had spent everything, there was a severe famine in that whole country, and he began to be in need. ¹⁵ So he went and hired himself out to a citizen of that country, who sent him to his fields to feed pigs. ¹⁶ He longed

to fill his stomach with the pods that the pigs were eating, but no one gave him anything." - Luke 15:14-16 (NIV)

Hitting bottom is usually an e_____ crisis for the prodigal.

17 "When he came to his senses, he said, 'How many of my father's hired servants have food to spare, and here I am starving to death! *18* I will set out and go back to my father and say to him: Father, I have sinned against heaven and against you. *19* I am no longer worthy to be called your son; make me like one of your hired servants.' *20* So he got up and went to his father." - Luke 15:17-20 (NIV)

When the prodigal repented, he came to his senses with:

- No s_____

- No p_____ involvement

- No m_____

His c_____ changed his heart.

On the prodigal's journey back home there was:

- No d_____

- No m_____

- No f_____ t_____ back home.

SESSION NOTES:

_____
_____
_____
_____
_____
_____
_____
_____

Homework

Give examples of how your prodigal has displayed beliefs and behaviors reflecting entitlement.

1. _____
2. _____
3. _____
4. _____
5. _____

The prodigal viewed his father as an object instead of as a soul so that the prodigal could get what he wanted.

Give examples of being used by your prodigal.

1. _____
2. _____
3. _____
4. _____
5. _____
6. _____
7. _____
8. _____

Often the prodigal has secret behavior even prior to the parents learning about them. Were there secrets or secret behaviors you learned later about your prodigal that were going on earlier? If so, list them.

1. _____
2. _____

3. _____
4. _____
5. _____
6. _____
7. _____
8. _____
9. _____
10. _____

What are some of the events that had to happen to the prodigal son for him to consider his condition?

_____
_____
_____
_____

Where was the prodigal when he repented?

_____
_____
_____
_____

The prodigal had to walk back home for weeks or months. What does this mean to you?

_____
_____
_____
_____

Problems for the Prodigal

DISC ONE: SESSION FIVE
LENGTH: 6 MINUTES 21 SECONDS

This session discusses the problems a prodigal gets into as a result of rejecting God.

When Israel rejected God as God they got into two primary problems.

    1. I_____

    2. Sexual I_____

Because of the thinking and behavioral problems, a prodigal, over time, can create one or more a_____.

If the prodigal has created an addiction, this could easily explain their:

- Crazy t_____

- Decision m_____

- Spiritual lack of m_____

When an active addiction starts, a person stops maturing:

- S_____

- M_____

- E_____

The patterns of addiction are:

    1. T_____ to stop the behavior

    2. Made p_____ to stop.

    3. They have c_____ for the behavior.

4. Keep u_____ even after the consequences.

5. Do m_____ and more of that behavior.

6. T_____ more to get the high.

7. Takes more t_____ for the behavior.

8. Go through w_____.

9. Less time for other a_____ or relationships.

SESSION NOTES:
_____
_____
_____
_____
_____
_____
_____
_____
_____

Homework

Give examples of your prodigal's potential immaturity in the following areas:

Spiritual:
_____
_____

Mental:
_____
_____

Emotional:
_____
_____

The patterns of addiction are:

1. Tried to stop the behavior.
2. Made promises to stop.
3. They have consequences for the behavior.
4. Keep using even after the consequences.
5. Do more and more of that behavior.
6. Takes more to get the high.
7. Takes more time for the behavior.
8. Go through withdrawals.
9. Less time for other activities or relationships.

Does your prodigal have three or more of these characteristics in their life?
_____

If you have answered yes to the last question, what are the behaviors, substances or relationships you might feel are addictive for your prodigal.

1._____
_____

2._____
_____

3._____
_____

4._____
_____

5. _____
_____

What are examples you have of believing that they might have an addiction issue?

_____
_____
_____
_____
_____
_____
_____
_____
_____

The Prodigal Parent Process can be one of the hardest and longest processes you might go through in your life. Do you feel these behaviors, substances, or relationships are becoming problematic for you? _____

If you have answered yes to the above question, write what or who you feel is becoming a medication for you in the process.

_____
_____
_____

If you feel you have crossed an addiction process in your life, what are your steps to get free from these behaviors, substances, or relationships?

_____
_____
_____

Secret Trauma

DISC ONE: SESSION SIX
LENGTH: 7 MINUTES 13 SECONDS

The percentage of sexual abuse and trauma is huge, even among Christians. This may possibly be a piece of your prodigal's journey whether or not they talk about it.

Statistically, sexual abuse will generally occur to:

One in _____ women

One in _____ men

Dr. Weiss discusses sexual trauma as not just an event or events. It is:

1. Move from trust to m_____

2. The m_____ they give the abuse

3. The way they act o_____

4. Feelings of w_____

5. Doubting that G_____ is real

Sexual trauma is often the d_____ secret of your prodigal, if this has occurred.

This is a question they are almost never a_____.

Write out the explanation of how to ask if someone has experienced sexual trauma.

_____
_____
_____
_____
_____

One more form of trauma that is common and needs to be addressed is a _____.

SESSION NOTES:
_____
_____
_____
_____
_____
_____
_____
_____
_____

Homework

Write out how you could ask your prodigal about potential sexual trauma.
_____
_____
_____
_____
_____

Have you had any secret trauma? _____

Have you talked about your secret trauma with someone? _____

If not, when will you? _____

If this is a part of you or your prodigal's journey, it is recommended to get professional help from a Christian counselor.

Sex

DISC ONE: SESSION SEVEN
LENGTH: 5 MINUTES 46 SECONDS

As a prodigal moves away from God, sex usually gets m_____.

> Flee from sexual immorality. All other sins a person commits are outside the body, but whoever sins sexually, sins against their own body. - I Corinthians 6:18 (NIV)

Our sexual reward system is the m_____ powerful reward system we have.

Unprotected sexuality is a w_____.

As a parent you did n_____ cause your prodigal's sexual choices.

Sexual choices are _____% the prodigal's responsibility.

SESSION NOTES:
_____
_____
_____
_____
_____
_____
_____
_____
_____
_____
_____

Homework

Sex is a very large topic in general. Sex, as it relates to a prodigal's journey, is very important for you as a parent of a prodigal to understand. We see poor sexual choices both in the prodigal son story and in Romans 1.

In your own words, write out what it means to sin against our own body.

_____
_____
_____
_____

What did you learn about how the human brain works during sex?

_____
_____
_____
_____

Sexual bonding is way more powerful than any bond in any relationship, including a child-parent bond.

Repeating <u>any</u> sexual behavior creates a neurological/psychological desire to repeat this behavior again.

In your own words, write out what this above statement means:

_____
_____
_____
_____

You may or may not know your prodigal's sexual choices. If you do know some of this, briefly describe how sex is playing a role in your prodigal's life.

_____
_____
_____
_____

Share why a prodigal could easily choose a sexual behavior or sexual partner over God, family, or even common sense.

_____
_____
_____
_____

Why are you not responsible for your prodigal's sexual choices?

_____
_____
_____
_____

Prodigals and Disorders

DISC ONE: SESSION EIGHT
LENGTH: 12 MINUTES 39 SECONDS

This session addresses disorders. These are separated into chemical imbalance disorders and psychological disorders.

Chemical disorder examples are:

    B_____I and II

    M_____ D_____

    S_____

You did not cause c_____ disorders.

Some causes for psychological disorders are surviving:

    A_____

    T_____

    N_____

The psychological disorders discussed in this session were:

    D_____

    B_____ Personality Disorder

    A_____

    N_____

SESSION NOTES:
_____
_____
_____
_____
_____
_____
_____
_____
_____
_____

Homework

Did any of the chemical imbalance disorder or psychological disorder symptoms seem to relate to your prodigal? If so, share them below:

_____
_____
_____
_____

If you feel your prodigal has any of these disorders, please research these and if they are willing, see a psychiatrist (not a general doctor) for a treatment strategy.

Are you able to pinpoint any times where your prodigal may have been abused, neglected, or experienced trauma? If so, list these instances below:

_____
_____
_____
_____

After watching depression symptom(s), do you have concerns about your prodigal? Why?

_____
_____
_____
_____

Also, be aware that low thyroid and low testosterone have similar symptoms. Before seeing a psychiatrist, get both a hormone panel and the thyroid evaluated, if they are willing.

Trust/Mistrust

DISC ONE: SESSION NINE
LENGTH: 11 MINUTES

This session adds more understanding of your prodigal's possible story that might be unknown to you. You are going to delve deep into your prodigal's heart to have a conversation about trust vs mistrust.

The prodigal process starts with m_____.

This statement is common for prodigals to say to Dr. Weiss:

"Doc, I don't t_____ anyone."

Mistrust and trust have k_____ outcomes.

Dr. Erik Erikson's Model of Human Development created in the 1950's identifies the following trust stages:

Stage 1:_____   Stage 5:_____

Stage 2:_____   Stage 6:_____

Stage 3:_____   Stage 7:_____

Stage 4:_____   Stage 8:_____

For those of us who trust, our lives get brighter and b_____.

Mistrust Stages:

Stage 1:_____   Stage 5:_____

Stage 2:_____   Stage 6:_____

Stage 3:_____   Stage 7:_____

Stage 4:_____   Stage 8:_____

It's not about you being trustworthy, it's about the prodigal being in a state of m_____.

SESSION NOTES:
_____
_____
_____
_____
_____
_____
_____
_____
_____

Homework

Write in your own words each stage of trust:

1. Trust
_____
_____

2. Authority
_____
_____

3. Initiative
_____
_____

4. Industry

_____
_____

5. Identity

_____
_____

6. Intimacy

_____
_____

7. Generosity

_____
_____

8. Integrity

_____
_____

Now, in your own words, describe each stage of mistrust:

1. Mistrust

_____
_____

2. Shame

_____
_____

3. Guilt

_____
_____

4. Inferiority

_____
_____

5. Role confusion

_____
_____

6. Isolation

_____
_____

7. Stagnation

_____
_____

8. Despair

_____
_____

How are some ways that your prodigal may feel about trust or mistrust:

_____
_____
_____
_____

In the below space, write out statements that you have heard your prodigal say that might be similar or indicate a heart that mistrusts.

1. _____
_____

2. _____
_____

3. _____
_____

4. _____
_____

5. _____
_____

6. _____
_____

7. _____
_____

8. _____
_____

9. _____
_____

10. _____
_____

When you closed your eyes and imagined all the mistrusting thoughts and the feelings that go along with that, what did you feel? Be sure to use feeling words only.

I felt:_____   I felt:_____

I felt:_____   I felt:_____

I felt:_____   I felt:_____

You know your prodigal better than most. What are some of the feelings that you think might be dominating their heart?

- _____   - _____

- _____   - _____

- _____   - _____

The prodigal's feelings are results of their choice or reaction to not trust? How have you seen this work in your prodigal's life?

_____

_____

_____

_____

This session ends by stating that trust reverses these consequences and can help your prodigal become more of who they can be. What are your thoughts about this?

_____

_____

_____

As a parent you can pray and ask God to help them heal their mistrust and to send people to them to help trust again.

In the biblical story of the prodigal son, the prodigal had to trust others for food, places to stay and sleep, and for water as he journeyed home. Each little step of trust helped him to trust his father when he finally arrived home.

The Will

DISC ONE: SESSION TEN
LENGTH: 6 MINUTES 32 SECONDS

Will is a very important topic in the dialogue about your prodigal. The use of the prodigal's will can help you add to your understanding of your prodigal's process.

The human will is the m_____ powerful force on Earth.

> And the Lord God commanded the man, "You are free to eat from any tree in the garden; - Genesis 2:16 (NIV)

What are the first three words God spoke to Adam?

"You are f_____"

The gift of choice is the most unique g_____ God has ever given in all eternity.

God knew his children could love him or r_____ him.

The will of your child is _____% theirs and not yours.

This is why you are 100% <u>not</u> r_____ for them choosing to be a prodigal.

The prodigal process is between God and t_____ only.

When God gave free will, He accepted fully that He was not r_____ for the choices of any individual.

SESSION NOTES:
_____
_____
_____
_____
_____
_____

Homework

Give examples of how the human will could be used for good:

- _____   - _____
- _____   - _____
- _____   - _____

Give examples of how the human will could be used for evil:

- _____   - _____
- _____   - _____
- _____   - _____

Who gets to decide how someone uses their own will? _____

What emotions do you feel when I speak about the fact that you cannot make your prodigal change?

_____
_____
_____
_____

The prodigal process is a "God and them" process only. Write what you think and feel about this statement.

_____
_____
_____
_____
_____

Object vs. Relational Thinking

DISC ONE: SESSION ELEVEN
LENGTH: 10 MINUTES 41 SECONDS

For although they knew God, they neither glorified him as God nor gave thanks to Him, but their thinking became futile and their foolish hearts were darkened. - Romans 1:21 (NIV)

In Proverbs, it talks about how a man thinks in his heart so is he. How a prodigal thinks is very important to understand. In working with prodigals of various types over the decades, I have learned that the soul has basically two operating systems; *object and relational thinking.*

I call the process of a prodigal who suppresses they truth they know self-b_____.

The reason someone betrays themselves is so they can d_____ what they want.

When they suppress the truth, they move away from r_____ thinking into o_____ thinking.

List the three principles of relational thinking:

    1. People have v_____

    2. There are r_____

    3. There are c_____

Do you think you are a relational thinker? If so, why? _____

List the three principles of object thinking:

1. People have n_____ value.

2. There are n_____ rules.

3. There should not be any c_____ for behaviors or choices.

SESSION NOTES:

_____
_____
_____
_____
_____
_____
_____
_____
_____
_____

Homework

When a prodigal continues in their process, they move to object thinking which is why they justify:

- Treating you poorly
- Yelling at you
- Stealing
- Lying to you

If these behaviors are occurring, your prodigal is treating you like you are an object. Upon coming to this realization, how does the fact that your child is participating in object thinking make you feel?

_____
_____
_____
_____

If you have examples of these types of behaviors or thought patterns from your prodigal, go ahead and write a few here:

1. _____
2. _____
3. _____
4. _____
5. _____

Give some examples of how you tried to rationalize or understand why your child was acting or thinking like this.

1. _____   4. _____
2. _____   5. _____
3. _____   6. _____

Object reality can continue until _____
_____
_____
_____

Starting Your Process

DISC TWO: SESSION ONE
LENGTH: 4 MINUTES 26 SECONDS

So far, we have focused on the prodigal process. I hope that has been helpful and freeing for you. Now, I want to focus biblically and practically on the Prodigal Parent Process. This session will focus on what you go through as a parent of a prodigal.

We have established that the prodigal process is _____% independent of the prodigal's parents.

The Prodigal Parent Process is very r_____.

The church in g_____ doesn't really address your pain.

Our next sessions are going to be:

    H_____

    V_____

My goal is to address the t_____ of having a prodigal child.

I want to give you l_____ for your Prodigal Parent Process.

SESSION NOTES:

_____
_____
_____
_____
_____
_____

Homework

Make a list of good Christian people you know personally who had less than wonderful or even ungodly parents, but they are serving Jesus with excellence.

1. _____   3. _____

2. _____   4. _____

List a few names of good, godly people who also have a prodigal. They can be Christian leaders or people you personally know:

1. _____   4. _____

2. _____   5. _____

3. _____   6. _____

Have you ever heard a sermon on the prodigal parents journey? If so, what did you learn?

_____

_____

_____

Trauma

DISC TWO: SESSION TWO
LENGTH: 4 MINUTES 08 SECONDS

Generally, Trauma is:_____
_____
_____

Having a prodigal child is like watching your child play r_____ r_____ with their lives.

The collective experiences the prodigal brings to you and your family can be t_____.

Trauma is a w_____ person trauma.

Trauma affect you:

    S_____

    S_____

    B_____

List a few of the impacts that the trauma and effects of having a prodigal child could have on you. Write the ones that apply to you:

1. _____
2. _____
3. _____
4. _____
5. _____
6. _____

Your excellence does not c_____ a known outcome.

SESSION NOTES:
_____
_____
_____
_____
_____
_____
_____
_____
_____
_____

Homework

Before watching this video, have you ever considered that parenting a prodigal can be traumatic? What are your thoughts now about the trauma this may have caused you?

1. _____
2. _____
3. _____
4. _____
5. _____
6. _____

Have you ever minimized the pain and impact this trauma has had in your life? If so, write out some examples here:

_____
_____
_____
_____
_____
_____
_____
_____

How do you believe your prodigal's choices have impacted your other family members?

_____
_____
_____
_____
_____
_____
_____
_____

How do you believe this Prodigal Parent Process has impacted your marriage?

_____
_____
_____
_____
_____
_____
_____

Everyone is Different

DISC TWO: SESSION THREE
LENGTH: 7 MINUTES 24 SECONDS

Trauma effects every couple d_____.

Symptoms of depression:

1. Feeling of w_____
2. Difficulty c_____
3. Difficulty making d_____
4. Weight g_____/l_____
5. Suicidal t_____
6. Low e_____
7. Sleep d_____
8. Feelings of h_____
9. Angry o_____
10. Loss of i_____ in pleasure, including sex

It's important as parents to take a look at ourselves in our healing journey. I have found that sometimes individuals or couples who are impacted by their prodigals may start to medicate their pain in unhealthy ways. This can include:

- Alcohol
- Social media
- Prescription drugs
- Overworking
- Television
- Getting into projects
- Food

Write down the characteristics of medications through a substance or behavior.

1. Tried to s_____
2. Made promises to s_____
3. Have C_____
4. Keep using after c_____
5. Use or do m_____
6. Takes m_____ for impact
7. Takes more t_____
8. W_____
9. D_____ in other activities

If you have more than three of these, evaluate this substance or behavior.

SESSION NOTES:

_____
_____
_____
_____
_____
_____
_____
_____
_____
_____

Homework

In this space, write out any of the symptoms of depression you feel you might be having.

1. _____
2. _____
3. _____
4. _____
5. _____
6. _____
7. _____
8. _____
9. _____
10. _____

In this space, write out the symptoms you are witnessing that your spouse is having in regards to depression.

1. _____
2. _____
3. _____
4. _____
5. _____
6. _____

It's important that you get a hormone panel and your thyroid checked before diagnosing yourself with depression. It's beneficial to have this completed before seeking medical or psychological help for depression so you can receive effective help.

Do you believe you need to address symptoms of depression you are having? If yes, write out a plan of action below.

_____
_____
_____
_____
_____

Circle ways that you may be medicating your pain:

Drugs	Prescription Drugs	Alcohol	Work	Social Media
Gaming	Shopping	Phone	Television	Exercise
Food	Caffeine	Sugar	Carbohydrates	Pornography

Medicating is a normal thing to do if you are in pain. Being a parent of a prodigal is painful.

If you have more than three of these, evaluate this substance or behavior.

If you believe you need to address any medicating habits you are having, write out a plan of action below.

_____
_____
_____
_____
_____
_____

Post Traumatic Stress Disorder

DISC TWO: SESSION FOUR
LENGTH: 11 MINUTES 42 SECONDS

Classic Post Traumatic Stress Disorder (PTSD) has to do with_____
_____
_____
_____

When you are in a primary relationship with someone who is putting the proverbial gun to their head, you can experience P_____.

There are 13 characteristics of PTSD that could relate to parents of a prodigal. List them here:

1. Having m_____, flashbacks or dreams.

2. Being t_____ or distressed.

3. A_____ plans, people and events.

4. N_____ about yourself or others in general.

5. H_____

6. P_____ away from other relationships.

7. D_____

8. Not e_____ activities

9. Challenges feeling P_____

10. M_____ issues

11. N_____ feelings

12. S_____ issues

13. Overwheling g_____ or shame.

If you are having some of these symptoms, it is suggested that you:

- See a t_____
- Talk to a same gender person in your Prodigal Parent G_____.

The Prodigal Parent Process is not about you, but it does i_____ you.

SESSION NOTES:

_____
_____
_____
_____
_____
_____
_____
_____
_____
_____

Homework

Have an honest moment with yourself. Review all 13 points and write out any of the PTSD symptoms you might be experiencing.

1. _____
2. _____
3. _____

4. _____
5. _____
6. _____
7. _____
8. _____
9. _____
10. _____
11. _____
12. _____
13. _____

If applicable, write out any PTSD symptoms your spouse potentially experienced in this process.

1. _____
2. _____
3. _____
4. _____
5. _____
6. _____
7. _____
8. _____
9. _____
10. _____
11. _____

12._____

13._____

Have you ever considered that managing/parenting a prodigal could cause PTSD symptoms? How are you feeling about this correlation?

_____
_____
_____
_____

Did evaluating these symptoms in your spouse help you start to recognize certain behaviors or reactions your spouse exhibits? If so, how do you better understand these behaviors?

_____
_____
_____
_____

If you believe that PTSD symptoms are playing a part in your marriage and/or life, how do you plan on addressing this moving forward?

Me:

_____
_____

My spouse:

_____
_____

Grief

DISC TWO: SESSIONS FIVE
LENGTH: 20 MINUTES 05 SECONDS

Many of us are familiar with the term grief. By now, you have likely gone through various forms of grief from a variety of different circumstances or even relationship loss. In this session, we are going to apply grief to the Prodigal Parent Process.

E_____ parent of a prodigal will go through grief.

Nine losses of the parents of prodigals:

1. The loss of who you t_____ they were.
2. The loss of your d_____ for them.
3. The loss of a "C_____" family.
4. The loss of seeing g_____.
5. The loss of r_____.
6. The loss of p_____ that all is well in your family.
7. The loss of e_____, time, resources and impact on your spouse and siblings.
8. The loss of f_____ events, holidays, birthdays.
9. The loss of having a prodigal are h_____ and sadly ongoing sometimes for decades.

Grief is a known p_____.

The stages of grief are:

1. S_____
2. D_____

Prodigal Parent Process Workbook | 63

3. A_____

4. B_____

5. S_____

6. A_____

Acceptance gets rid of:

1. F_____ guilt

2. B_____

3. False s_____

Acceptance keeps you free from t_____ you are going to make the difference.

Acceptance allows you to trust G_____.

You can't a_____ grief.

Understanding grief can help you be compassionate toward y_____ and your _____.

SESSION NOTES:

_____
_____
_____
_____
_____
_____
_____
_____
_____
_____

Homework

As you look at the list of the various losses, write down the five that most impacted you here:

1. _____
2. _____
3. _____
4. _____
5. _____

Each situation is different. Are there any losses you can think of for yourself that were not listed in the video? If so, please write these here:

1. _____
2. _____
3. _____
4. _____
5. _____

I strongly encourage you to make a time to share these with your spouse, a good friend of the same gender, or someone in your Prodigal Parent Group.

Did you have a "wake up call" when you discovered your child is not who you think they are? Write out your wake-up call moment:

_____
_____
_____
_____
_____

In the following spaces, in your own words, describe each stage of grief:

Shock:
_____
_____

Denial:
_____
_____

Anger:
_____
_____

Bargaining:
_____
_____

Sadness:
_____
_____

Acceptance:
_____
_____

In the below spaces, give examples from your journey with your prodigal.

Shock:
_____
_____
_____
_____

Denial:

_____
_____
_____
_____

Anger:

_____
_____
_____
_____

Bargaining:

_____
_____
_____
_____

Sadness:

_____
_____
_____
_____

Acceptance:

_____
_____
_____
_____

Although you will go up and down through the various stages of grief, you could primarily be in one stage for a season. As you evaluate these stages of grief, what stage do you feel you're currently in and why?

_____
_____
_____
_____

In the acceptance session of grief, I mention seven acceptance statements. In the below spaces write how you currently feel, think, or believe about each statement. Please be brutally honest with yourself as you experience these statements today.

1. My child is in rebellion against God.

_____
_____
_____

2. My child is playing by their own rules.

_____
_____
_____

3. My child does not value our values or us.

_____
_____
_____

4. My child has done this to themselves.

_____
_____
_____

5. My child can't understand our pain or the pain they create in our family.

_____
_____
_____

6. My child is a prodigal from God and until that changes not much can be expected to change.

_____
_____
_____

7. My child being a prodigal is not my or my spouse's fault.

_____
_____
_____

In your mind and heart how much today do you believe these seven statements?

_____%

As you both walk through the various stages of grief, I strongly recommend you have a friend of the same gender that you share your grief process with. Grief is processed much better when you don't grieve alone.

My person of the same gender to walk with through grief is:_____

Anger

DISC TWO: SESSION SIX
LENGTH: 9 MINUTES 37 SECONDS

Anger is a very common feeling for prodigal parents; however, the feeling of anger is complicated because you love this person who is damaging people you love. In this session we want to discuss what you can do about the legitimate anger you could easily have toward your prodigal.

Some parents of prodigals have a real c_____ admitting they have anger.

Of course you would be angry if you were:

1. "Treated like an o_____"

2. "M_____"

3. "Let d_____ repeatedly"

God got angry at I_____ on more than one occasion.

Your anger is l_____ and a_____ to be angry.

This session walks through three points on the Cleansing the Temple account in the Gospel. They are:

1. I _____ the sin

2. Engage his anger p_____

3. Temple was c_____

You know you are that t_____.

Your prodigal behavior and choices have d_____ your life.

Only y_____ can clean your temple.

The Cleansing the Temple process:

1. Write an a_____ letter

2. Read it o_____ loud

3. Get a b_____ / racquet and mattress

4. W_____ up

5. Go b_____

It's very important to get the r_____ out of your body.

SESSION NOTES:
_____
_____
_____
_____
_____
_____
_____
_____
_____
_____
_____
_____

Homework

On a separate tablet, write your anger letter.

The date I wrote my letter was on (date):_____

Negotiate a time to be alone in the home and do the Cleansing the Temple exercise.

The date I did the actual cleansing of my temple was on (date):_____

*If you have any *physical* or *heart conditions*, seek a medical doctor's approval prior to doing this exercise.

What were some of the key things you were angry about in your letter to your prodigal?

_____
_____
_____
_____

During the anger work, what else came up that was important or different from your letter?

_____
_____
_____
_____

After you did the Cleansing of the Temple exercise, how did you feel?

_____
_____
_____
_____

If you have put this off more than a week, who can you be accountable to weekly until you do this exercise?

Name:_____

Forgiveness

DISC TWO: SESSION SEVEN
LENGTH: 8 MINUTES 34 SECONDS

Christian forgiveness is a key idea of our faith. Forgiveness is an ongoing aspect when you are a parent of a prodigal.

I highly recommend you complete the C_____ the Temple exercise before doing the Forgiveness exercise in this session.

In the below spaces, write out the three myths of forgiveness in your own words.

1. _____
   _____

2. _____
   _____

3. _____
   _____

The benefits of doing the forgiveness exercise are:

1. You can do it a_____
2. You don't need the p_____ cooperation
3. You can keep your h_____ clean

SESSION NOTES:
_____
_____
_____
_____

Prodigal Parent Process Workbook | 73

_____
_____
_____
_____
_____

Homework

What does true forgiveness mean to you?
_____
_____
_____

Have you struggled with forgiving your prodigal for their offenses or pain they have caused you and/or your loved ones?
_____
_____
_____

After completing the forgiveness exercise, write out your experience:
_____
_____
_____

What benefits did this exercise have for you spiritually and/or emotionally?
_____
_____
_____

Cause and Effect

DISC TWO: SESSION EIGHT
LENGTH: 5 MINUTES 14 SECONDS

Cause and effect beliefs can prolong many of the impacts your prodigal is having in your life.

Even as an i_____ we learn cause and effect.

We are rewarded and have consequences largely by c_____ and effect.

If I am a good parent, I s_____ have good Christian children.

Because of free will, outcomes are:

    1. U_____

    2. U_____

Your job as a parent is to:

    1. Create the e_____

    2. I_____

    3. D_____

    4. D_____

    5. P_____ the best you can

You are not responsible for o_____.

Free will totally e_____ the possibility of cause and effect.

If you keep "shoulding" on yourself you can:

    1. Stay s_____ chasing a lie.

2. Suffer u_____

When we agree our children have a free will, we, like God can:

   1. Create an e_____

   2. Establish e_____

   3. Allow c_____

   4. Allow c_____

What percentage of God's first two children became prodigals? _____%

SESSION NOTES:

_____
_____
_____
_____
_____
_____
_____
_____
_____
_____
_____
_____

Homework

In your own words, write out what your deepest fear is as a parent:
_____
_____
_____
_____

What do you think about the fact that God does not hold you accountable for your child's free will?
_____
_____
_____
_____

Powerless

DISC TWO: SESSION NINE
LENGTH: 5 MINUTES 53 SECONDS

The term *powerless* has helped millions of recovering people accept reality as it is. As a parent of a prodigal, accepting, as we discovered in the grief session, is very important.

Powerless means without p_____.

Because our children have free will, we do not have p_____ to make them chose anything.

Every parent wants this power; if the parent does X then the child will c_____.

When you grasp you are powerless, you are in r_____.

The great thing about being powerless is you are free from o_____.

SESSION NOTES:

_____
_____
_____
_____
_____
_____
_____
_____
_____
_____
_____
_____

Homework

What feelings come up for you when you admit you are powerless over your prodigal?

1. _____   3. _____

2. _____   4. _____

List a few other ideas you are free from when you accept you are powerless.

1. _____   4. _____

2. _____   5. _____

3. _____   6. _____

When you closed your eyes and said I am powerless over _____ (prodigal's name) what did you experience?

_____
_____
_____
_____

If this is an area of struggle, I would recommend you say the prayer suggested in this session:

"LORD, I am powerless over my prodigal and I turn them fully over to You. I trust You, not myself, to help them see how good You are."

Proverbs 22:6

DISC THREE: SESSIONS ONE
LENGTH: 8 MINUTES 14 SECONDS

Whenever you get into a conversation with a parent of a prodigal, it is very common for them to quote Proverbs 22:6. No conversation about prodigals or the parents of prodigals would be complete without discussing this verse.

> Train up a child in the way he should go: and when he is old, he will not depart from it. - Proverbs 22:6 (KJV)

This verse is h_____ for many parents of prodigals.

As a parent you:

1. T_____ lessons

2. Read s_____

3. Show a Christian l_____

4. Plant good s_____

Dr. Weiss has seen t_____ of prodigals return back to God.

As a parent, you give your children a G_____ to know where God is.

A prodigal returning can take d_____.

As parents, we can't make the t_____ of their repentance happen on our schedule.

Dr. Weiss is sharing that some prodigals come home in their 50s, 60s, and even later. Why is he sharing this with you? To e_____ you.

The scripture says when they are o_____.

SESSION NOTES:
_____
_____
_____
_____
_____
_____
_____
_____

Homework

As a parent, you can't bend scripture. What does this mean in the context of Proverb 22:6?

_____
_____
_____

As a parent, you want the prodigal to turn away from their sinful ways as soon as possible. What are some feelings that arise when you realize this timing is something you have no control over?

_____
_____
_____

List an example of a celebrity or someone you know who was living as a prodigal but returned to his or her faith.

_____
_____
_____

Almost Never

DISC THREE: SESSION TWO
LENGTH: 7 MINUTES 03 SECONDS

The Prodigal Process

Step One: An external event happens to the prodigal. Write out a few examples that may occur:

- _____
- _____
- _____

Step Two: This external event creates an i_____ crisis for the prodigal.

Step Three: The external crisis leads to an internal crisis that leads to two changes.

1. Hardening of the h_____

2. Shifting toward G_____

What is not in this process? _____

Parents are r_____ involved in the prodigal coming back to God.

Who are some of the people Dr. Weiss suggests could be a part of your prodigal coming home to God?

- _____
- _____
- _____

You do not have to feel p_____ to be that person.

82 | Prodigal Parent Process Workbook

Let G_____ decide the set of circumstances or people that brings them back home.

SESSION NOTES:
_____
_____
_____
_____
_____
_____
_____
_____
_____
_____
_____
_____

Homework

Has your prodigal ever had an external event occur? If so, write a few examples:
_____
_____
_____
_____

The external event creates internal crisis. Give general examples of this:
_____
_____
_____
_____

Give examples of internal existential crisis:

_____
_____
_____
_____

To your knowledge has your prodigal had an internal crisis? If so, share these on the according topics:

Existential:

_____
_____
_____

Pragmatic:

_____
_____
_____

Remember, when you take on a responsibility that God has not given you, it can drain and impact you and your marriage.

The Father's Behavior

DISC THREE: SESSION THREE
LENGTH: 5 MINUTES 25 SECONDS

Earlier your attention has been on the prodigal. As you are moving through the Prodigal Parent Process, we will review two clear prodigal accounts, but from the father's perspective.

> ¹¹ Jesus continued: "There was a man who had two sons. ¹² The younger one said to his father, 'Father, give me my share of the estate.' So, he divided his property between them. ¹³ "Not long after that, the younger son got together all he had, set off for a distant country and there squandered his wealth in wild living." ¹⁴ "After he had spent everything, there was a severe famine in that whole country, and he began to be in need. ¹⁵ So he went and hired himself out to a citizen of that country, who sent him to his fields to feed pigs. ¹⁶ He longed to fill his stomach with the pods that the pigs were eating, but no one gave him anything." ¹⁷ "When he came to his senses, he said, 'How many of my father's hired servants have food to spare, and here I am starving to death! ¹⁸ I will set out and go back to my father and say to him: Father, I have sinned against heaven and against you. ¹⁹ I am no longer worthy to be called your son; make me like one of your hired servants.' ²⁰ So he got up and went to his father. ²¹ "The son said to him, 'Father, I have sinned against heaven and against you. I am no longer worthy to be called your son.' ²² "But the father said to his servants, 'Quick! Bring the best robe and put it on him. Put a ring on his finger and sandals on his feet. ²³ Bring the fattened calf and kill it. Let's have a feast and celebrate. ²⁴ For this son of mine was dead and is alive again; he was lost and is found.' So to celebrate. - Luke 15:11-24 (NIV)

In the Luke story, let's pick up after the father gave the son the resources and the son left.

This section discusses the "nevers" of the father. In the below space, write these in your own words.

1. The father never:_____

2. The father never:_____

3. The father never:_____

4. The father never:_____

5. The father stayed on the p_____.

6. The father kept the environment of the house s_____.

7. As a parent of a prodigal, the hardest thing to do is t_____ the process.

²¹ The Lord God made garments of skin for Adam and his wife and clothed them. ²² And the Lord God said, "The man has now become like one of us, knowing good and evil. He must not be allowed to reach out his hand and take also from the tree of life and eat, and live forever." ²³ So the Lord God banished him from the Garden of Eden to work the ground from which he had been taken. ²⁴ After he drove the man out, he placed on the east side of the Garden of Eden cherubim and a flaming sword flashing back and forth to guard the way to the tree of life.- Genesis 3:21-24 (NIV)

In the Genesis story, there are three points about the Father's behavior. In your own words, write out these ideas.

1._____

2._____

3._____

God allowed natural c_____ for their behavior.

As you go through this process, you being in a_____ with your spouse is really important.

SESSION NOTES:
_____
_____
_____
_____
_____
_____
_____
_____
_____
_____
_____

Homework

What are you gleaning from the father's behavior toward the prodigal in Luke 15?
_____
_____
_____
_____
_____

In your own words, write out what it meant for this father to stay on the porch:
_____
_____
_____
_____
_____

What would it mean for you to "stay on the porch" for your prodigal?

_____
_____
_____
_____

As you look at God and also the prodigal father's behavior, what are principles that you take away that could be helpful in your journey with your prodigal?

_____
_____
_____
_____

Boundaries

DISC THREE: SESSIONS FOUR
LENGTH: 8 MINUTES 26 SECONDS

Boundaries are very important in the prodigal process. In the last session, we saw that both sets of fathers had really good boundaries.

Boundaries with prodigals can be a c_____.

Boundaries can be a place where your m_____ can be injured if not in agreement.

One parent can be more s_____ and the other more p_____ based.

It is important to:

    1. E_____ boundaries with your prodigal.

    2. Agree upon them t_____.

    3. K_____ the boundaries.

If boundaries are violated, bring in a t_____ person.

The primary boundaries for the parents of prodigals to discuss are:

    1. M_____

    2. T_____

    3. E_____

    4. F_____

What is important in boundaries is that:

    1. You a_____

    2. You stick to your a_____

A spouse that has s_____ in dealing with the prodigal is preferring their emotions and the prodigal over their s_____.

P_____ is the quickest way back to God; not r_____ from pain.

It is not l_____ to keep someone from hitting bottom.

Just because it's good doesn't mean it's G_____.

SESSION NOTES:
_____
_____
_____
_____
_____
_____
_____
_____
_____
_____
_____
_____

Homework

In your own words, write out how a soft parent might want to address the prodigal's issues as they come up?
_____
_____
_____

In your own words, write out how a principled parent might want to address the prodigal's issues as they come up?

_____
_____
_____

Which approach do you most identify with?

_____
_____

Which approach do you believe your spouse takes?

_____
_____

Do you believe your current approach is the approach you want to continue with? Why or why not?

_____
_____
_____
_____

If one of the parents break agreed upon boundaries, it is beneficial to have a third person walk with you both through the Prodigal Parent Process. Who can that person be that you both could be honest and accountable to? You both must be in agreement with who this person is.

_____

Write a couple of agreed upon primary boundaries in each section:

Money:

_____
_____

Time:
_____
_____

Events:
_____
_____

Friends:
_____
_____

What does it mean when a spouse is keeping secrets?
_____
_____
_____

What are your thoughts on this statement: *"It is not loving to keep someone from hitting rock bottom."*
_____
_____
_____
_____
_____

The Siblings

DISC THREE: SESSION FIVE
LENGTH: 14 MINUTES 30 SECONDS

If your prodigal has siblings, they are very likely impacted by the decisions the prodigal is making. Not only does it impact them as a sibling, but they see it impact you and the entire family dynamics.

The siblings (in your own words):

1. Watch _____

2. Listen to _____

3. Hear _____

The siblings also hear y_____ cry.

They not only carry their p_____ from the prodigal, they carry the pain of watching how you are being t_____.

When a sibling watches how a parent is treated, oftentimes, resentment builds up toward the prodigal and this causes the sibling to feel r_____.

> [25] "Meanwhile, the older son was in the field. When he came near the house, he heard music and dancing. [26] So he called one of the servants and asked him what was going on. [27] 'Your brother has come,' he replied, 'and your father has killed the fattened calf because he has him back safe and sound.' [28] "The older brother became angry and refused to go in. So his father went out and pleaded with him. [29] But he answered his father, 'Look! All these years I've been slaving for you and never disobeyed your orders. Yet you never gave me even a young goat so I could celebrate with my friends. [30] But when this son of yours who has squandered your property with prostitutes comes home, you kill the fattened calf for him! - Luke 15:25-30 NIV)

One of the resentments of the sibling is that he had to do m_____, not less because of the prodigal.

The sibling needed more t_____ to see change.

The sibling restoration process can take l_____.

The father a_____ the son.

The father v_____ the son.

The father h_____ the sibling prodigal process.

For the sibling it's not so much about forgiveness as it is about t_____.

SESSION NOTES:

_____
_____
_____
_____
_____
_____
_____
_____
_____
_____
_____

Homework

In the story of the prodigal, the brother knew his brother's issues before he left. It is quite possible that the siblings know more of the behind-the-scenes story of your prodigal than you do.

In your situation, did your other children end up telling you more information about your prodigal's story? If so, write a little about what you learned from your other children.

_____
_____
_____
_____
_____

How do you feel or think about the sibling's need to see proof before re-engaging the prodigal (be honest)?

_____
_____
_____
_____
_____

Due to the prodigal's decisions, many non-prodigal siblings feel resentment and feelings of being robbed. Have you noticed this in any of your non-prodigal children? If so, list some examples of this below:

_____
_____
_____
_____

What is the last thing the non-prodigal siblings need from you?

_____
_____
_____

Write out what it would sound like if you were genuinely validating the pain of the other sibling(s):

_____
_____
_____
_____
_____
_____

What could happen if you push your "happy family" picture on the other siblings?

_____
_____
_____
_____
_____
_____
_____

Taking Responsibility

DISC THREE: SESSION SIX
LENGTH: 7 MINUTES 06 SECONDS

"Where did I go wrong?" "What did I do?" "I wasn't a perfect parent." All of these, and so many other questions and statements come up when you are going through the trauma of having a prodigal child. Some of these questions/statements can be coming from the bargaining stage of grief, but some of these statements may feel or actually be legitimate concerns.

From the prodigal's perspective, during counseling m_____ do not blame their parents for their choices.

There are parents who have created p_____ for their prodigal.

Make a list of regrets you have and how the prodigal could have felt.

Regrets you have:

1._____
2._____
3._____
4._____
5._____

How the prodigal could have felt:

1._____
2._____
3._____
4._____
5._____

How to take responsibility with your prodigal:

- Make an appointment with your prodigal in a p_____ place.
- Take responsibility and go over each i_____ separately.
- Ask for f_____

Three points about having zero expectations are:

1. This is not m_____ bullet to bring them back.

2. This is not a g_____ that anything will change.

3. It is you m_____ taking responsibility for the areas of parenting that you feel you need to take responsibility.

SESSION NOTES:

_____
_____
_____
_____
_____
_____
_____
_____
_____
_____
_____
_____

Homework

The possible pain a parent could have created is broken down into sections. If applicable, fill in this possible pain below:

Physical abuse:

_____
_____

Physical neglect:

_____

_____

Emotional abuse:

_____

_____

Emotional neglect:

_____

_____

Sexual abuse:

_____

_____

Sexual neglect:

_____

_____

Spiritual abuse:

_____

_____

Spiritual neglect:

_____

_____

Were the above behaviors also done to other siblings?_____

You may be carrying false or legitimate guilt over very specific things you said or didn't say, did or didn't do. If so, list these:

1. _____
_____

2. _____
_____

3. _____
_____

4. _____
_____

5. _____
_____

6. _____
_____

7. _____
_____

8. _____
_____

9. _____
_____

10. _____
_____

In this session, I advised you to make a list of things you need to take responsibility for on the left and what your prodigal could have felt on the right.

The date I finished my list was: _____/_____/_____

Before going to meet with your prodigal to take ownership of your list, it is suggested that you have a supportive person of the same gender to talk to afterwards.

The name of this person is: _____

In the below space, write out your experience talking to your prodigal.

_____
_____
_____
_____
_____
_____
_____
_____
_____
_____
_____
_____
_____
_____
_____

The date I completed this with all my children was: _____/_____/_____

Forgiving Us

DISC THREE: SESSION SEVEN
LENGTH: 4 MINUTES 20 SECONDS

In the last segment, we discovered that, as parents, none of us are perfect. We have all sinned. The scripture is clear about this. This session covers an aspect of the Prodigal Parent Process about forgiving.

In your own words, write out the Chair Exercise.

_____
_____
_____

The C_____ exercise can help you to forgive yourself.

It may be also helpful for you to do the chair exercise with G_____.

If you can forgive yourself you are not going to come from a place of _____ guilt.

SESSION NOTES:

_____
_____
_____
_____
_____
_____
_____
_____
_____

Homework

Set a date and time to do the chair exercise:

_____/_____/_____ at_____ AM / PM

What did you experience in the first chair when asking for forgiveness from yourself?

_____
_____
_____
_____

What did you experience in the second chair when responding to your request to be forgiven?

_____
_____
_____
_____

What did you experience the second time in the first chair responding to yourself?

_____
_____
_____
_____

Blaming

DISC THREE: SESSION EIGHT
LENGTH: 3 MINUTES 25 SECONDS

There is a dynamic of blame that can occur in any marriage while trying to manage having a prodigal child. At this point in our study, it's important to again recognize and understand that 100 % of the prodigal's choice is the prodigal's choice, not your spouses.

Describe the "context" that you both are experiencing as a parent of a prodigal:

_____
_____
_____
_____

You know your spouse is n_____ responsible for your prodigal's choices.

The prodigal process is between G_____ and your child, not your p_____.

Do not let your prodigal get in the way of your m_____.

SESSION NOTES:
_____
_____
_____
_____
_____
_____
_____

Homework

Give examples of an "If you…" blaming statement that you have thought of or actually said to your spouse in your process thus far:

1. _____
   _____

2. _____
   _____

3. _____
   _____

4. _____
   _____

5. _____
   _____

6. _____
   _____

7. _____
   _____

8. _____
   _____

Make a list of regrets you have and how the spouse could have felt:

Regrets you have: How your spouse could have felt:

1._____   1._____

2._____   2._____

3._____   3._____

4._____   4._____

5._____   5._____

What did you realize while making this list of regrets toward your spouse?

_____

_____

_____

_____

I will take responsibility for my behaviors and statements on the following date:

_____/_____/_____

What did you experience after you finished taking responsibility with your spouse?

_____

_____

_____

_____

The Marriage

DISC THREE: SESSION NINE
LENGTH: 7 MINUTES 34 SECONDS

Marriage was the final creation of God in the garden. This organic triune unit is amazing, complete, and beautiful, yet it can be significantly impacted, bruised, and injured by a Prodigal Parent Process gone poorly.

These are some of the impacts both of you could be having as a result of the trauma of having a prodigal:

D_____

P_____

A_____

G_____

False g_____

If the marriage structure is not m_____ the marriage can get weaker than it needs to be while going through the Prodigal Parent Process.

In your own words, describe these marriage structure ideas:

Spiritual:

_____
_____

Dating:

_____
_____

Social:

_____
_____

Feelings:

_____
_____

Sex:

_____
_____

Finances:

_____
_____

A steady diet of m_____ books is recommended.

SESSION NOTES:

_____
_____
_____
_____
_____
_____
_____

Homework

Keeping your marriage strong during your Prodigal Parent Process is critical to maintaining a great Christian marriage.

In the below spaces, write out your commitments in each area.

Spiritual:

1. _____
2. _____
3. _____

Dating:

1. _____
2. _____
3. _____

Social:

1. _____
2. _____
3. _____

Feelings:

1. _____
2. _____
3. _____

Sex:

1._____

2._____

3._____

Finances:

1._____

2._____

3._____

A way to guarantee you keep your marriage strong is to hold yourselves accountable to a pastor or another couple during your Prodigal Parent Process.

That couple or person's name is:_____

My Hope

DISC THREE: SESSION TEN
LENGTH: 6 MINUTES 27 SECONDS

There are several ideas that I hope you learned during these sessions:

1. _____
2. _____
3. _____
4. _____
5. _____
6. _____
7. _____
8. _____
9. _____

SESSION NOTES:
_____
_____
_____
_____
_____
_____
_____
_____
_____
_____
_____

Homework

In the below section, write out what your hope is for yourself in this process:
_____
_____
_____
_____
_____
_____
_____
_____

In the below space, write out what your hope is for your marriage in this process:
_____
_____
_____
_____
_____
_____
_____
_____

I am so very proud of you for walking through all these sessions. As you know, there are millions of prodigals, many in your own church. I encourage you to reach out to them and share your knowledge and experiences.

While your journey, as well as your prodigal's, is still unfolding, my hope is that by completing this series you are more equipped than ever before as you move forward as a prodigal parent. Through this teaching you have learned that your prodigal has a free will of their own and you are not responsible for the choices your prodigal has made. You have learned about boundaries and how to enforce them. You have also learned that, if you're married, your spouse's emotions and grief process are important as well and prioritizing and investing into your marriage is imperative as you both navigate this season. Additionally, we dove deep into what medicating pain looks like and the potential trauma you may have endured as a prodigal parent. Furthermore, you were given several beneficial therapeutic exercises and advice that could help you navigate these trying times. I am hopeful that this information has been valuable in your healing process.

Resources for parents of prodigals are few and far between. If you're able, I recommend sharing some of the information you have learned from the *Prodigal Parent Process* with other parents of prodigals who are struggling. If you feel called to help other parents in this situation, feel free to register a Prodigal Parent Support group with my team at 719-278-3708. Churches are lacking this fundamental space for prodigal parents and the vital information you can bring through a support group can help bridge this gap. I additionally want to encourage you to join my support forum on Facebook for parents of prodigals – all of whom are at different points of their journey – at www.facebook.com/groups/prodigalparents.

Again, I want to applaud you for investing in yourself as a parent of a prodigal and encourage you to anchor yourself in the truth, Christ, and His Word as you await the return of your prodigal child.

appendix

PARENTS OF PRODIGALS
facebook group

You are not alone in your journey. We are here to support, encourage & pray with you as you await the return of your prodigal child.

JOIN US!

WWW.FACEBOOK.COM/GROUPS/PRODIGALPARENTS

MARRIAGE RESOURCES

LOVER SPOUSE

Lover Spouse helps you understand marriage from a Christ-centered perspective. Christian Marriages were designed to be different, passionate, fulfilling, and long-lasting.   BOOK: $13.95

UPGRADE YOUR SEX LIFE

Upgrade Your Sex Life actually teaches you own unique sexual expression that you and your partner are pre-wired to enjoy.
BOOK: $16.95

SERVANT MARRIAGE

Servant Marriage book is a Revelation on God's Masterpiece of marriage. In these pages, you will walk with God as He creates the man, the woman and his masterpiece called marriage.
BOOK: $13.95

MARRIAGE MONDAYS

This is an eight week marriage training that actually gives you the skills to have a healthy and more vibrant marriage.

DVD: $59.95

INTIMACY

This 100 Day guide can transform couples from any level of intimacy to a lifestyle of satiation with their spouse.   BOOK: $11.99

MIRACLE OF MARRIAGE

God made your marriage to be an amazing and unique miracle. Dr. Weiss walks you through the creation and maintenance of your marriage. You will be exposed to a practical insights that can help make your marriage into God's original design.
BOOK: $12.95

OTHER RESOURCES

WORTHY: EXERCISES & STEP BOOK

The *Worthy* Workbook and DVD, is designed for a 12 week study. Here is a path that anyone can take to get and stay worthy. Follow this path, and you too will make the journey from worthless to worthy just as others have.

DVD: $29.95
BOOK: $29.95

EMOTIONAL FITNESS

Everyone has an unlimited number of emotions, but few have been trained to identify, choose, communicate, and master them. More than a guide for gaining emotional fitness and mastery, in these pages you will find a pathway to a much more fulfilling life.

BOOK: $16.95

LETTERS TO MY DAUGHTER

A gift for your daugher as she enters college. *Letters to my Daughter* includes my daily letters to my daughter during her first year of college.

BOOK: $14.95

BORN FOR WAR

Born for War teaches practical tools to defeat these sexual landmines and offers scriptural truths that empower young men to desire successfulness in the war thrust upon them.

DVD: $29.95

PRINCES TAKE LONGER THAN FROGS

This 2 hour DVD helps single women ages 15-30, to successfully navigate through the season of dating.

DVD: $29.95

SUCCESSFULLY SINGLE

This 2 Disc DVD Series is definitely nothing you have heard before. Dr. Weiss charts new territory as to the why for sexual purity.

DVD: $29.95

INTIMACY ANOREXIA

This hidden addiction is destroying so many marriages today. In your hands is the first antidote for someone with intimacy anorexia to turn the pages on this addiction process. Excerpts from intimacy anorexics and their spouses help this book become clinically helpful and personal in its impact to communicate hope and healing for the intimacy anorexic and the marriage.

BOOK: $22.95
DVD: $69.95

INTIMACY ANOREXIA: THE WORKBOOK

This is like therapy in a box. Inside is 100 exercises that have already been proven helpful in treating intimacy anorexia.

WORKBOOK: $39.95

INTIMACY ANOREXIA: THE STEPS

This is the only twelve step workbook just for intimacy anorexia. Each step gives you progress in your healing from intimacy anorexia.

STEP BOOK: $14.95

MARRIED & ALONE

This is for the spouse of an intimacy anorexic. You feel disconnected, untouched and often unloved. You are not crazy and Dr. Weiss will help you to start a journey of recovery from living with a spouse with intimacy anorexia.

BOOK: $14.95
DVD: $49.95

MARRIED & ALONE: HEALING EXERCISES FOR SPOUSES

This is the first workbook to offer practical suggestions and techniques to better navigate through recovery from your spouse's Intimacy Anorexia.

WORKBOOK: $39.95

MARRIED & ALONE: THE TWELVE STEP GUIDE

This Twelve Step guide will help the spouse of an intimacy anorexic work through the Twelve Steps that many others have found to be helpful in their recovery.

STEP BOOK: $14.95

SERIES FOR MEN

CLEAN

BOOK: $16.95
DVD: $29.95
JOURNAL: $16.95

Every Christian man is born into a sexual war. The enemy attacks the young, hoping to scar them permanently and leave them ruined. Your past is not enough to keep you from the enduringly clean life you want and deserve. This series can be used individually or in a small group setting.

LUST FREE LIVING

Every man can fight for and obtain a lust free lifestyle. Once you know how to stop lust, you will realize how weak lust really can be. God gace you the power to protect those you love from the ravages of lust for the rest of your life! It's time to take it back!

BOOK: $13.95
DVD: $23.95

MEN MAKE MEN

Dr. Weiss takes the listeners by the hand and step-by-step walks through the creative process God used to make every man into a man of God. This practical teaching on DVD combined with the Men Make Guidebook can revitalize the men in any home or local church.

DVD: $29.95
GUIDEBOOK: $11.95

MEN'S RECOVERY

This book gives more current information than many professional counselors have today. In addition to informing sex addicts and their partners about sex addiction, it gives hope for recovery. The information provided in this book would cost hundreds of dollars in counseling hours to receive. Many have attested to successful recovery from this information alone.

BOOK: $22.95
CD: $35.00

101 FREEDOM EXERCISES

This is the best single resource for the Christian who desires to know what they need to do to get and stay free from sexual addiction. This book contains 101 exercises that have been proven to work.

WORKBOOK: $39.95

STEPS TO FREEDOM

This is a Christian approach to the Twelve Steps. This book will guide you through the 12 Steps of recovery that have been helpful for many addicted people. This book is specifically written for the person desiring recovery from sexual addiction.

STEP BOOK: $14.95

HELPING HER HEAL

The *Helping Her Heal* DVD is for the man who has disclosed his sexual addiction to his partner or spouse. This DVD offers practical tools for hearing her pain, navigating her grief and losses, discovering her expectations of you and the boundaries she may need to heal.

DVD: $69.95

MARRIED AFTER ADDICTION

Addiction can have devastating effects on even good marriages. In this DVD you are intelligently guided through the journey you will experience if addiction is part of your marriage story. You will learn important information about the early and later stages of recovery for your marriage.

DVD: $29.95

WOMEN'S RECOVERY

Partners: Healing From His Addiction book is the latest in research of the affects on a woman who has lived with a sexual addict. The riveting statistics combined with personal stories of recovery make this a must read book for any woman in a relationship with a sex addict. This book gives you hope and a beginning plan for personal recovery.

BOOK: $14.95

PARTNER'S RECOVERY GUIDE

This is like therapy in a box for women who want to walk through the residual effects of being in a relationship with a sex addict.

WORKBOOK: $39.95

BEYOND LOVE

This is an interactive workbook that allows the partners of sex addicts to gain insight and strength through working the Twelve Steps.

STEP BOOK: $14.95

HE NEEDS TO CHANGE, DR. WEISS

He Needs To Change, Dr. Weiss DVD addresses the pain, trauma, and betrayal women experience because of their partner's sex addiction, betrayal, and/or intimacy anorexia. In this DVD, Dr. Weiss addresses the issue of change that he has explained to thousands of women in his office.

DVD: $29.95

UNSTUCK FOR PARTNERS

The *Unstuck* DVD is for every woman who has experienced the pain of their partner's sex addiction or intimacy anorexia and feels stuck, confused, frustrated and unable to move on. You didn't sign up for this and honestly, you don't get it! This DVD helps you "get it" so you can process the painful reality you are in and start to live again.

DVD: $29.95

PARTNER BETRAYAL TRAUMA

Partner Betrayal Trauma is real. Your pain and experience of betrayal has impacted all of your being and all of your relationships.

The book, DVD set, Workbook and Step guide were designed to help guide you thoughtfully through your own personal healing from the effects of being betrayed by your spouse or significant other. The pain and trauma of being betrayed, especially sexual betrayal, by a spouse or significant other is multidimensional and multifaceted. Your pain and trauma are real and these resources will help you in your journey of recovery from Partner Betrayal Trauma.

BOOK: $22.95   DVD: $65.95   WORKBOOK: $39.95   STEPBOOK: $14.95

RECOVERY RESOURCES

Recovery for Everyone helps addicts fight and recover from any addiction they are facing. Learn truths and gain a biblical understanding to break the strongholds in your life.

You will also find an explanation as to how an addiction may have become a part of your life and details as to how you can walk the path to recovery. You will find a roadmap to help you begin and navigate an incredible journey toward freedom. Then you can become part of the solution and even help others get free as well.

BOOK: $22.95   DVD: $99.00   WORKBOOK: $39.95   STEPBOOK: $14.95

RESOURCES FOR FEMALE SEX ADDICTS

Secret Solutions is a practical recovery exercise workbook written specifically for female sex addicts. Many of these techniques have been used in private practice to help other female sex addicts.

WORKBOOK: $39.95

She has a Secret book is the most current book in the field of sex addiction for women and is packed with new statistics to further our understanding of female sexual addiction. This is a must-read for any woman struggling in this addiction as well as for professionals in this field.

BOOK: $14.95

Heart to Heart Counseling Center has recently acquired Cereset, the most technologically advanced neuromodulation software available. It has received 13 peer review publications, and 9 Institutional Review Boards (IRB) clinically approved trials including the US Military.

By rebalancing and recalibrating the brain, it has helped anxiety, PTSD, trauma, sleeplessness, addiction, low mood and energy, TBI, stress management and neuroplasticity in many of my clients. Most spouses at Heart to Heart Counseling Center have many of the PTSD symptoms from betrayal. More than 80% of those with addiction have unresolved traumas as part of their story.

The brain is your central command center. When your brain is out of balance, or stuck, you don't feel right and it's impossible to function at your highest level. Cereset is a proven technology that's non-invasive and highly effective. Cereset can help your brain free itself, enabling you to achieve higher levels of well-being and balance throughout your life.

Here's what clients had to say about Cereset Garden of the Gods after their sessions:

> "I'm waking up earlier and feeling more rested and alert. Anxiety is lessened. PTSD symptoms alleviated. Lessened food cravings and quantity of food reduced. Arthritis symptoms improved. I feel more relaxed, less angry and reactive."

The cost for five sessions (one per day) is $1,500.

For more information call us at 719-278-3708

A·A·S·A·T
American Association for Sex Addiction Therapy

SEX ADDICTION TRAINING SET

Both men and women are seeking to counsel more than ever for sexually addictive behaviors. You can be prepared! Forty-seven hours of topics related to sexual addiction treatment are covered in this training including:
- The Six Types of Sex Addicts
- Neurological Understanding
- Sex and Recovery
- Relapse Strategies

TRAINING SET: $1195

PARTNER'S RECOVERY TRAINING SET

With this AASAT training, you will gain proven clinical insight into treating the issues facing partners. You can be prepared! Thirty-nine hours of topics related to partners treatment are covered in this training, including:
- Partner Model
- Partner Grief
- Anger
- Boundaries

TRAINING SET: $995

INTIMACY ANOREXIA TRAINING SET

This growing issue of Intimacy Anorexia will need your competent help in your community. Now, you can be prepared to identify it and treat it. In this training you'll cover topics like:
- Identifying Intimacy Anorexia
- Causes of Intimacy Anorexia
- Treatment Plan
- Relapse Strategies

TRAINING SET: $995

FOR MORE INFORMATION VISIT WWW.AASAT.ORG OR CALL 719.330.2425

NEW PRODUCTS

NARCISSISM SEX ADDICTION AND INTIMACY ANOREXIA

The profound information that you will learn in this DVD will help you fairly evaluate your specific situation for narcissism, which will help you develop a treatment plan to address the issue you are dealing with at its core. Having this clarity can help expedite the healing process for the sex addict, intimacy anorexic, and the spouse, as they are able to tackle the real issue at hand.

DVD: $29.95

DISCLOSURE

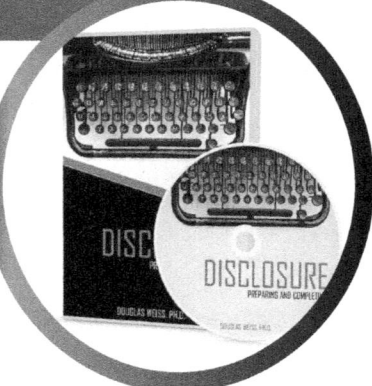

Disclosure is one of the most important topics in sexual addiction recovery. In this DVD, Dr. Weiss discusses the various types of disclosure. Each type of disclosure is for a specific purpose or person. This DVD can expedite the understanding of each of the significant processes of disclosure for the addict, the spouse and the marriage.

DVD: $39.95

BOUNDARIES

Boundaries are a healthy, normal, and necessary part of the recovery process for sex addicts, intimacy anorexics, and their spouses. In this DVD set, Dr. Doug Weiss provides an answer to the clarion call on boundaries by educating and guiding you through this process.

DVD: $49.95

SIN OF WITHHOLDING

This DVD is the first to address the Biblical foundation of the sin of withholding in believers' hearts. The practical application in marriage addressing Intimacy Anorexia is also interwoven in this revelational teaching on the Sin of Withholding. Once a believer is free of this sin, their walk with the Lord and their fruit towards others can increase expediently.

DVD SET: $49.95

PAIN FOR LOVE

Pain For Love describes in detail one of the most insidious strategies of an intimacy anorexic with their spouse. This dynamic is experienced by many who are married to an intimacy anorexic. This paradigm can empower the spouse and help them stop participating in a pain for love dynamic in their marriage.

DVD: $29.95

HEALING HER HEART AFTER RELAPSE

Relapse doesn't have to occur, but if it happens, knowing how to navigate it intelligently can make a huge difference in a marriage. Each relapse impacts the wife significantly.

This DVD is way more than, "He relapses, he does a consequence and moves on." The addict is given real tools to address the emotional damage and repair of her heart as a result of a relapse. Every couple in recovery would do well to have these tools before a potential relapse.

DVD: $29.95

Made in the USA
Columbia, SC
30 July 2022